VOLUME FOUR

Part One: Jesus the King

Part Two: Heaven Speaks to Priests

Part Three: Jesus Speaks to Sinners

Direction for Our Times
As given to Anne,
a lay apostle

VOLUME FOUR

Direction for Our Times
As given to Anne, a lay apostle

ISBN-13: 978-0-9766841-3-8

Library of Congress Number: Applied For

Publisher:
Direction for Our Times
9000 West 81st Street
Justice, IL 60458
708-496-9300
www.directionforourtimes.org

Direction for Our Times is a 501(c)(3) tax-exempt organization.

Manufactured in the United States of America

Graphic Design: Pete Massari

Direction for Our Times wishes to manifest its complete obedience and submission of mind and heart to the final and definitive judgment of the Magisterium of the Catholic Church and the local Ordinary regarding the supernatural character of the messages received by Anne, a lay apostle.

In this spirit, the messages of Anne, a lay apostle, have been submitted to her bishop, Most Reverend Leo O'Reilly, Bishop of Kilmore, Ireland, and to the Vatican Congregation for the Doctrine of the Faith for formal examination. In the meantime Bishop O'Reilly has given permission for their publication.

October 11, 2004

Dear Friends,

I am very much impressed with the messages delivered by Anne who states that they are received from God the Father, Jesus, and the Blessed Mother. They provide material for excellent and substantial meditation for those to whom they are intended, namely to the laity, to bishops and priests; and sinners with particular difficulties. These messages should not be read hurriedly but reserved for a time when heartfelt recollection and examination can be made.

I am impressed by the complete dedication of Anne to the authority of the magisterium, to her local Bishop and especially to the Holy Father. She is a very loyal daughter of the Church.

Sincerely in Christ,

Philip M. Hannan

Archbishop Philip M. Hannan, (Ret.)
President of FOCUS Worldwide Network
Retired Archbishop of New Orleans

PMH/aac

106 Metairie Lawn Dr. • Metairie, LA 70001 • Phone(504) 840-9898 • Fax(504) 840-9818

Dr. Mark I. Miravalle, S.T.D.
Professor of Theology and Mariology, Franciscan University of Steubenville
313 High Street • Hopedale, OH 43976 • U.S.A.
740-937-2277 • mmiravalle@franciscan.edu

Without in any way seeking to anticipate the final and definitive judgment of the local bishop and of the Holy See (to which we owe our filial obedience of mind and heart), I wish to manifest my personal discernment concerning the nature of the messages received by "Anne," a Lay Apostle.

After an examination of the reported messages and an interview with the visionary herself, I personally believe that the messages received by "Anne" are of supernatural origin.

The message contents are in conformity with the faith and morals teachings of the Catholic Church's Magisterium and in no way violate orthodox Catholic doctrine. The phenomena of the precise manner of how the messages are transmitted (i.e., the locutions and visions) are consistent with the Church's historical precedence for authentic private revelation. The spiritual fruits (cf. Mt. 7:17-20) of Christian faith, conversion, love, and interior peace, based particularly upon a renewed awareness of the indwelling Christ and prayer before the Blessed Sacrament, have been significantly manifested in various parts of the world within a relatively brief time since the messages have been received and promulgated. Hence the principal criteria used by ecclesiastical commissions to investigate reported supernatural events (message, phenomena, and spiritual fruits) are, in my opinion, substantially satisfied in the case of "Anne's" experience.

The messages which speak of the coming of Jesus Christ, the "Returning King" do not refer to an imminent end of the world with Christ's final physical coming, but rather call for a spiritual receptivity to an ongoing spiritual return of Jesus Christ, a dynamic advent of Jesus which ushers in a time of extraordinary grace and peace for humanity (in ways similar to the Fatima promise for an eventual era of peace as a result of the Triumph of the Immaculate Heart of Mary, or perhaps the "new springtime" for the Church referred to by the words of the great John Paul II).

As "Anne" has received permission from her local ordinary, Bishop Leo O'Reilly, for the spreading of her messages, and has also submitted all her writings to the Congregation for the Doctrine of the Faith, I would personally encourage, (as the Church herself permits), the prayerful reading of these messages, as they have constituted an authentic spiritual benefit for a significant number of Catholic leaders throughout the world.

Mark I. Miravalle

Dr. Mark Miravalle
Professor of Theology and Mariology
Franciscan University of Steubenville
October 13, 2006

Table of Contents

Introduction

Dear Reader,

I am a wife, mother of six, and a Secular Franciscan.

At the age of twenty, I was divorced for serious reasons and with pastoral support in this decision. In my mid-twenties I was a single parent, working and bringing up a daughter. As a daily Mass communicant, I saw my faith as sustaining and had begun a journey toward unity with Jesus, through the Secular Franciscan Order or Third Order.

My sister travelled to Medjugorje and came home on fire with the Holy Spirit. After hearing of her beautiful pilgrimage, I experienced an even more profound conversion. During the following year I experienced various levels of deepened prayer, including a dream of the Blessed Mother, where she asked me if I would work for Christ. During the dream she showed me that this special spiritual work would mean I would be separated from others in the world. She actually showed me my extended family and how I would be separated from them. I told her that I did not care. I would do anything asked of me.

Shortly after, I became sick with endometriosis. I have been sick ever since, with one thing or another. My sicknesses are always the types that mystify doctors in the beginning. This is part of the cross and I mention it because so many suffer in this way. I was told by my doctor that I would never conceive children. As a single parent, this did not concern me as I assumed it was God's will. Soon after, I met a wonderful man. My first marriage had been annulled and we married and conceived five children.

Spiritually speaking, I had many experiences that included what I now know to be interior locutions. These moments were beautiful and the words still stand out firmly in my heart, but I did not get excited because I was busy offering up illnesses and exhaustion. I took it as a matter of course that Jesus had to work hard to sustain me as He had given me a lot to handle. In looking back, I see that He was preparing me to do His work. My preparation period was long, difficult and not very exciting. From the outside, I think people thought, man, that woman has bad luck. From the inside, I saw that while my sufferings were painful and long lasting, my little family was growing in love, in size and in wisdom, in the sense that my husband and I certainly understood what was important and what was not important. Our continued crosses did that for us.

Various circumstances compelled my husband and me to move with our children far from my loved ones. I offered this up and must say it is the most difficult thing I have had to contend with. Living in exile brings many beautiful opportunities to align with Christ's will; however, you have to continually remind yourself that you are doing that. Otherwise you just feel sad. After several years in exile, I finally got the inspiration to go to Medjugorje. It was actually a gift from my husband for my fortieth birthday. I had tried to go once before, but circumstances prevented the trip and I understood it was not God's will. Finally, though, it was time and my eldest daughter and I found ourselves in front of St. James Church. It was her second trip to Medjugorje.

I did not expect or consider that I would experience anything out of the ordinary. My daughter, who loved it on her first trip, made many jokes about people looking for miracles. She affectionately calls Medjugorje a carnival for religious people. She also says it is the happiest place on earth. This young woman initially went there as a rebellious fourteen-year-old, who took the opportunity to travel abroad with her aunt. She returned calm and respectful, prompting my husband to say we would send all our teenagers on pilgrimage.

At any rate, we had a beautiful five days. I experienced a spiritual healing on the mountain. My daughter rested and prayed. A quiet but significant thing happened to me. During my Communions, I spoke with Jesus conversationally. I thought this was beautiful, but it had happened before on occasion so I was not stunned or overcome. I remember telling others that

Communions in Medjugorje were powerful. I came home, deeply grateful to Our Lady for bringing us there.

The conversations continued all that winter. At some time in the six months that followed our trip, the conversations leaked into my life and came at odd times throughout the day. Jesus began to direct me with decision and I found it more and more difficult to refuse when He asked me to do this or that. I told no one.

During this time, I also began to experience direction from the Blessed Mother. Their voices are not hard to distinguish. I do not hear them in an auditory way, but in my soul or mind. By this time I knew that something remarkable was occurring and Jesus was telling me that He had special work for me, over and above my primary vocation as wife and mother. He told me to write the messages down and that He would arrange to have them published and disseminated. Looking back, it took Him a long time to get me comfortable enough where I was willing to trust Him. I trust His voice now and will continue to do my best to serve Him, given my constant struggle with weaknesses, faults, and the pull of the world.

Please pray for me as I continue to try to serve Jesus. Please answer "yes" to Him because He so badly needs us and He is so kind. He will take you right into His heart if you let Him. I am praying for you and am so grateful to God that He has given you these words. Anyone who knows Him must fall in love with Him, such is His goodness. If you have been struggling, this is your answer. He is coming to you in a special way through these words and the graces that flow through them.

Please do not fall into the trap of thinking that He cannot possibly mean for you to reach high levels of holiness. As I say somewhere in my writings, the greatest sign of the times is Jesus having to make do with the likes of me as His secretary. I consider myself the B-team, dear friends. Join me and together we will do our little bit for Him.

Message received from Jesus immediately following my writing of the above biographical information:

You see, My child, that you and I have been together for a long time. I was working quietly in your life for years before you began this work. Anne, how I love you. You can look back through your life and see so many "yes" answers to Me. Does that not please you and make you glad? You began to say "yes" to Me long before you experienced extraordinary graces. If you had not, My dearest, I could never have given you the graces or assigned this mission to you. Do you see how important it was that you got up every day, in your ordinary life, and said "yes" to your God,

despite difficulty, temptation, and hardship? You could not see the big plan as I saw it. You had to rely on your faith. Anne, I tell you today, it is still that way. You cannot see My plan, which is bigger than your human mind can accept. Please continue to rely on your faith as it brings Me such glory. Look at how much I have been able to do with you, simply because you made a quiet and humble decision for Me. Make another quiet and humble decision on this day and every day, saying, "I will serve God." Last night you served Me by bringing comfort to a soul in pain. You decided against yourself and for Me, through your service to him. There was gladness in heaven, Anne. You are Mine. I am yours. Stay with Me, My child. Stay with Me.

The Allegiance Prayer For All Lay Apostles

Dear God in heaven, I pledge my allegiance to You. I give You my life, my work and my heart. In turn, give me the grace of obeying Your every direction to the fullest possible extent. Amen.

Part One:
Jesus the King

January 8, 2004
Jesus

My children in this world of darkness, your salvation is at hand. I, Jesus Christ, return to collect for the Father what is rightfully His, namely, His children. The last time I walked your earth I was a man. My earthly origins were humble, as befitted the One who had come to serve. My origins on this, My return, are majestic. I come as King. I am the King of All Peoples. I come not to redeem you, but to lead you. I am the ruler of the world and in that capacity I will rule this world and its inhabitants. The time of darkness ends now. The faithful must rejoice as their time has come. Sinners, repent, during this brief time of grace. You must decide. Do you serve the light? Or will you continue in darkness? You have been warned. You have been urged. Darkness holds nothing for you. Choose light now. All has been foretold. Mankind turned away from Me. But mankind can no longer turn away. I burst through the darkness now in all glory. Be at peace and sing praise to the Almighty, for truly, God's Kingdom comes.

January 9, 2004
Jesus

Children of the world, look toward the light. Raise your eyes to all that is goodness. I come to you with joy and celebration. The time for mourning is past because God has taken His children back to His breast, never to be parted. This world, your world, has suffered. Sin obscured the light until children began to doubt the very existence of God. This will never be allowed to happen again. God, in all His omniscience, allowed mankind to direct itself and direct the course of humanity so that he could see the fruits of separation from heaven. Children, with all of the wisdom of heaven, you can now see the level of darkness that settled in ever growing layers upon the world. Prophets from even one hundred years ago could never have imagined such evil. They could not fathom the depravity that would be accepted by men of the future. The enemies of heaven have persuaded humanity that much of this evil is good. We have visited those absurdities and need dwell no longer on them because I have come. I am leading you to the light that never changes. There will not be a new light tomorrow. God is and will be.

He is eternal. His laws have no need of adaptation to new generations, children, because they are the guides for all humans, given the inclinations that can draw man from God. Women of the world, rejoice. Your salvation is at hand. Your children's children will be joyful followers of the light. Have no fear that your world spins out of control. God's sustaining hand is directing all. Pray with confidence that all has been allowed for the triumph of heaven and of heaven's children. If you experience grief, know that I will wipe away every tear. You will be comforted with divine comfort if you ask Me. Heaven and earth are joined together to usher in the New Time. All is well, dear humanity. All is well.

January 10, 2004
God the Father

I give greetings to My children on this earth. It is I, your Father in heaven, who speaks to you. My children, you are participating in a time of change. The saints in heaven only wished they could have lived in this time. It is similar to the time when Jesus was born in Bethlehem. You might say the world is with child again because the world is awaiting the return of the Savior. Jesus loves this world and Jesus loves each one of you tenderly. I will not even discuss the love that I hold for each of you because it is understood that a Creator, when He creates something as precious and perfect as each one of you, loves the created. You are the created, children of heaven. You did not accidentally arrive on earth due to a series of biological events. This is nonsense. The biological event that was your birth caused all of heaven to let out their breath in expectation of your time in the world. I created you to bring My Kingdom on earth that much closer to the return of My Son. You are to participate in this joyous process. You must ask Me, your God, what plan I have for your participation. Some will reject Me, of course. I am well used to that during this age of disobedience. So perhaps I might ask you to serve Me in all love and allegiance to compensate for those who reject Me. Will you do that for Me, My little souls? Please have no fears. Understand that the Father wills these changes on earth so that the Son will be welcomed in the hearts of those remaining. We do not manifest as a poor boy in the stable. We manifest as the King of Creation. My Son is your God. I am your God. Our Spirit flows through your world in such a way today that none can deny the heavenly times. The enemy will deny Our Spirit. But you expect that, dear ones. That denial detracts in no way from truth. Truth flows right over the enemy despite the feeble objections of evil. I, the God of All Creation, can slap down and destroy evil with a glance. I allow a certain amount of evil to co-exist because My children can then discern between light and darkness, in the same way a child is taught to discriminate between cold and hot. Children, if you desire to blame Me for the state of the world, your ancestors in heaven will bow their heads in disappointment. Do not be so ridiculous. I do not will catastrophe upon My children. I do allow a certain amount of upheaval so that attention will be focused away

from the ever present diversion of material goods. In line with this goal, I will begin to remove many material comforts. Consider this a liberating experience, earthly creatures. Your losses on earth are nothing in comparison to the loss you will experience if you choose darkness. Be humble and accepting in everything and together We will prepare the world for the return of My Son.

January 12, 2004
God the Father

Children of the world, be consoled. Hardship during your time on earth is to be expected. Be peaceful about the difficulties that come your way. Look to Me for consolation. Tell Me your difficulties and I will comfort you in a way that defies human understanding. Remember that when all was going well, when you had many material possessions and advantages, you also had unhappiness. It is important that you retain a heavenly perspective now, during this time of difficulty. I want to share My view with you. From heaven, where I monitored the fall of every leaf, I saw a world that was unbalanced. Some of My children had every possible earthly possession. Because of the abundance of such possessions, My children in some parts of the world began to think in a distorted way. They thought then that they were entitled to such riches. When they could not secure the riches they admired, they began to think they were deprived. They became unhappy, much as a child who has had too many treats will get sick and feel unwell and stop laughing and smiling. A child who indulges in too many treats sickens himself, which is why a parent is careful to control the amount of treats a child ingests. My children in the more affluent areas of the world experienced this occurrence and their unhappiness and dissatisfaction led to all manner of spiritual decay. My heavenly view shifts for a moment and I gaze upon other areas of the world, where during this same time, children lay dying of starvation and disease, simply for the want of basic necessities. These are the two extremes. They are equally disturbing to Me because I neither created one group to be gluttonous or the other to live and die in misery. Children, were you the father of this group of individuals, what would you do? You would, like Me, say, "Enough. We must restructure. The Father's riches must be more equitably distributed." Now there are many good and just souls in the first group who share their wealth and have always done so. You will be rewarded far beyond your ability to imagine. You have understood the injustice. You have assisted your holy brothers and sisters who have selflessly gone to minister to the unfortunates in God's family. And for the souls who have given their lives to Me in the spirit of missionary work? I need not discuss here what is to be their reward. What limit can there be on the gratitude of the God Grateful? All that I have is available to these merciful servants. Please accept My peace as I create a world that is healthy for all of God's children. You will be happier, My dear ones, when the rule of Jesus Christ has been established on earth. What difference is it to you as long as your eternity is secured? I want joy, now, for all. If you do not feel joy, if you experience the sorrows of the world, know that it is temporary and that My plan is for your spiritual safety and salvation.

January 13, 2004
God the Father

My children of the world, I would like you to ask Me for everything you need. I am your Father and in this time I seek to be available to each one of you in a clear way. Ask Me for what you require and I will see that you have it. You are accustomed to fulfilling every need through the world. In this way, you forgot to look toward heaven. Now you will look to heaven again and that is as it should be. Cry out to your Father, who sees all and takes all into consideration. You will become dependent on Me as past generations were dependent on Me. This is natural and holy. This is the way I designed your world. Independence is good in that you do not rely on other men. But you are designed to be reliant on your God. This is not a negative dependence but a respectful attitude of understanding who is the Master of All Creation. Am I a despotic King, to be despised? Am I to be resented for My authority? Would you pay Me false homage to please Me because you fear My retaliation? This is the way people worship false gods, dear children. People worship the one true God by obeying through love and respect. I am worthy of all love and respect. I am worthy of your love. I have always proved Myself to be the greatest friend of mankind and when you die and I hold you in My arms, you will understand that you owed Me fidelity while you were on earth. I will console you for your failures, children. You will then understand that I did not expect perfection and that My love for you is eternal and compassionate. What joy you will have, dear one, in being reunited with Me. In view of all of this, I am asking for your faith and service, as I always have. But I am asking in a special way that you trust Me and put Me in the first place. 'Should we follow this path? Let us ask God, our Father. Should we follow another path? Certainly not without consulting God, our Father. We are in trouble and require this or that material thing for our sustenance. Let us immediately, and with great confidence, beseech our Father in heaven to provide this thing. He has created us, therefore He will care for us.' Children, you look to the starving in areas of your world and say, "But look, He did not take care of those children." I would respond to you that I arranged for their care but My more affluent children did not share their gifts. So the failure was not Mine, but My children's. In this new age of obedience, most of the children on

earth will be obedient to Me and in this way, I will be able to work through them effectively. Children, there will be great joy on earth. And souls on earth will clearly understand that they are working toward heaven through their actions on every day. Children, this is a beautiful way to live. This is the way I intended you to live. And I designed your time on earth to be peaceful and educational, not miserable. So exult, oh favored ones. You live in a time when your God is returning. How often have My holy children wailed in despair and said, "God, why do You allow this evil to continue?" Well, My servants, I allow it no longer.

January 14, 2004
God the Father

My children in this changing world, I want you to know that I am with you. I tell you this often, in many ways, because if you give consideration to the thought that your God is present in all that occurs, you will not feel frightened. How can a soul be afraid when the all-powerful, all-knowing Father is present, watching each situation, and through each situation, bringing about the best possible outcome for that soul? You do not see Me, it is true, but again I make reference to the wind, which makes its presence felt in its effects. I am that way also. You know I am present by the effect I have on you, on the situation where I am called in, and on the souls who respond to My presence within you. You see, My children in the world, I use each one of you to bring Me and present Me to others. If you are respectful of Me, if you acknowledge My dominion over you and your world, I am with you. In this way, I can be brought everywhere. I can be present to any soul who is with you. I can manifest Myself in many ways. I manifest Myself in your patience. I manifest Myself in your love for another when you ordinarily would find it difficult to love that person. I am present in your smile, in your speech, and I am present in your decisions, which is very important. So you do not see Me, it is true, but you will feel the difference if you go either from serving Me to not serving Me, or from not serving Me to serving Me. Serve Me now and let us no longer have any lapses in service. Remain with Me, your heavenly Father, who seeks to direct all that has an impact on you. I will bring every event in your life and turn it into something that benefits your soul and gives you eternal satisfaction and joy. But not all in my life is good, you are thinking. I know that, My child. That is why you need Me. I can turn the pain, the anguish, the mistakes and grief, into strength, wisdom, patience, and joy. Truly, if you are detached from the world and from worldly things, you can experience a foretaste of heaven on earth, and then you will have less desire for earthly things. You will have a clearer, more defined focus. You will have less difficulty with the idea of leaving the earth and making the journey to your home in heaven. Believe Me when I tell you that everything I say, all that I share with you, I share with you for your own benefit. I am your Father and a Father sees to the needs of His children. Use Me, children, to calm your spirit and direct your path. It is for this reason that I come to you now.

January 15, 2004
Jesus the King

My brothers and sisters of the world must prepare their hearts to welcome their King. In past times when groups of humanity were ruled by kings, all would prepare for the return of their ruler following his absence. Well, I have been away from your world in the physical sense for many years. Now I prepare to return. I am ready. Your world is not. What must you do to be ready? My brothers and sisters in the world must prepare their hearts. How do you want Me to find you when I come back? Would you be so immersed in the world that My return will be an unpleasant and shocking interruption to your worship of the false gods of materialism and sensuality? That will not be good for you, dear soul, because you will not understand or fully experience the joy that is rightfully yours. You must prepare to claim that joy. You must set an example of peaceful and watchful readiness. When I find you, you will want to welcome Me in all recollected holiness. Do I demand that you become a saint overnight? My little soul, of course I do not. This is not even possible for you. I do not expect it. Like a welcomed and beloved guest, I look not at how high you have reached spiritually, but how willing you are to work with Me on your soul. I am looking for a calm acceptance that you are My subject and live in My Kingdom. You will be lifted up in My Kingdom. You will be one of My close advisors and friends who, upon My return, will bring Me all manner of news and requests. You will say, "Lord, God of this world, all is not well with this soul. This soul needs your special help." Because you are My faithful one, the souls whom you recommend will have My special help and also My special mercy. You will say also, "Lord, God of this world, I would like to see Your influence more strongly in this school, this hospital, this church, this religious order, this political group." I will say, "Good idea, servant of the King. You shall have what you request, because you are My faithful subject who waited for Me in faith and love." Do you see how we will spread My Kingdom? You will not be spit upon any longer. You will have the power that is heaven propelling My ways throughout your world. I have selected you and placed you right where you are so that you would be available to bring Me where I need to go. Prepare your heart, My beloved servant. I am coming. I will

scatter the darkness with one wave of My arm. Evil will cower in vain, as I see all. There will be no more hiding behind the guise of goodness. Now in all joy, in all gratitude, prepare your heart to receive Me.

January 16, 2004
Jesus the King

My brothers and sisters, I give you these words so that you are prepared for My return. It is with great joy that I come to you now. I have seen the pain in this world and it is My greatest consolation to know that I am going to alleviate this pain and bring peace and joy into hearts and homes again. Can you imagine the distress I have felt, watching souls as they wandered through a loveless world? Most souls did not understand that they had only to ask for divine companionship and such companionship awaited them. Most souls did not understand that their fellow souls in the world suffered from a form of spiritual sickness that spread like a ghastly contagion through the world. They felt they were unloved because they were unlovable, when in reality, those who were placed in their lives to love them, were also suffering. This situation has intensified until even parents began to love themselves more than their own children. These children grew into adulthood lacking self-worth and example. They were then not capable of parenting their own children. Your Jesus has suffered through this, willingly assisting any and all who remembered that the Heavenly Physician could help. How relieved I was when a soul would turn to Me in desperation and request assistance. I lavished all graces on that soul and when that soul's loved ones would accept My graces, I lavished all graces upon his loved ones. In cases where his loved ones would not accept My graces, I consoled My faithful follower until his loved one was ready to accept My help. Make no mistake, dear ones, your Jesus has not sat idly by while your world suffered. I pleaded with the world through every possible avenue. The world has rejected Me. This has happened in the past, as I have told you, but not to this same degree. Because of that, heaven chooses to act in an unparalleled manner. The process of My return has begun. You are the avenues through which these graces will flow. Open your hearts to Me now, little souls of the Kingdom. Watch in amazement how My Spirit flows through you. You need do nothing exceptional except be open to My will. I will do everything. When you feel pressure, it is because you are attempting to do My work for Me. Who could do the work of God? Certainly not a little learning soul who is attempting to find perfection in a very imperfect world. Let Me work through

you. Let Me love you and support you as I make the necessary changes in your soul that will allow Me to flow through you uninhibited. All is well, My beloved children. You need worry over nothing.

January 17, 2004
Jesus the King

My brothers and sisters must remain where I have placed them, in all calm, and in all trust. It is through you that I return, at least in this initial phase. You are listening to My words, You are experiencing My spirit within you, and you are preparing to assist heaven. This is good. I would like you to also do one other thing. I would like you to begin walking with Me in earnest. My beloved servants, I have told you that I am with you. I have told you that I will never leave you. If I am at all welcomed by you, I reside within you. But I am also beside you. I am in every conversation where someone asks Me to participate. Do you want to know how to please Me? Allow Me to speak through you. Allow Me to act through you. Allow Me to love through you. You have noticed changes since you began to follow Me with decision. You have noticed that as the world attempts to pull you away from peace, I draw you back to peace. You have noticed that it is easier to love those around you. You have noticed more patience, more joy, and a deeper contemplation of the world as I see it. Now, little souls, I want you to begin practicing something different. I want you to calmly bring Me with you in everything you do and everything you say. In each part of each day, understand that I, the King of heaven and earth, am working through you. You must notice that I often use the word calm. I refer to calmness and the spirit of calm. Why do I do this? Because often My children get excited and that is not from Me. How will you change because I work through you? You will be quieter, more thoughtful; you will smile more and frown less. You will overlook the flaws of your brothers and sisters as I overlook yours. I will align your priorities so that your priorities are directly influenced by My priorities. My beloved soul, try for a moment to imagine a world populated by souls such as yours. This is going to occur. My Father has willed this and it will come about, gradually at first, and then more quickly. You, My soul whom I have watched so closely, are a part of this. You have a role to play. I need you and you are Mine. Do not think that this will be difficult for you. It will be the most natural, most comfortable, and most wonderful state of being you have ever experienced. My true followers, who have aligned their will to Mine, already understand this state of being and they are at peace. You, too, will

have such a peace. Be joyful, now, dear ones. All is well and God is firmly directing all.

January 19, 2004
Jesus the King

Dearest children in the world, you are afraid. I wish to alleviate fear entirely from your lives. Followers of the light should never fear because man cannot diminish My light. If you carry Me within you, there is nothing that can hurt your eternity. I will protect My Spirit within you and that is the only thing that should concern you, the loss of My Spirit. In this time of change, you must walk in the light with determination. Children do not often fear because they rely on their parents for everything. When they face a problem, they run to their parents and place the problem with their parents, running off again to continue with their childlike pursuits. Take heed, dear ones. This is what we ask of you at this time. And we ask this for your own peace. This is the way to proceed during this time of change and transition. Soon, it will come naturally to you and you will have no need to remind yourself each day. I have asked My children to practice their faith and by that I mean continued acts of trust when trust would seem difficult and there is a temptation toward fear and distress. You must say, "I have given this to my

Father in heaven. God wants to protect me so I will take full advantage of my Parentage and allow Him to do so. In this way, I am mentally liberated and can do the work my Father wills for me in freedom. My concentration should be on each task that is placed in front of me, never worrying about the past, never worrying about the future. Only in the present can I serve my God and my God needs my service." Would you say, "No, God, I cannot serve You now as I must sit down and worry about tomorrow. Find someone else to do Your work while I busy myself with this worrying"? My brothers and sisters, your God has not asked you to worry this day. He has planned many tasks for you today and worrying is not among those tasks. Worrying and distressing yourself is your will for yourself, not God's will for you. A true servant, and I want each one of you to be true servants, is joyful because he or she only wants to serve God in the present. This servant knows that in the present God's will is being accomplished and this servant is a part of heaven by the commitment he or she has made. What else can you ask for, little ones? You are on the straight path to heaven. Should you be taken from that path at any time, you will simply complete your ascent effortlessly because I will be there to lift you the remainder of the way. In other words, as long as you stay on the path, there is nothing, nothing, that should have the power to upset you. Your eternity is secured. Do you understand? You will lose everything from this world eventually. That is for certain as when you lie down to die, you bring nothing with you but your service to God. If you are united to Me, your Jesus who loves you, I will stand before you and justice and your sins will be blown away like so many small embers from a fire. For this day, I ask that you simply concentrate on what it is God is asking of you right now. That is My request, little ones. Focus on serving God's Kingdom today.

January 20, 2004
Jesus the King

Brothers and sisters, sing praise to the Father, whatever the circumstances of your time on earth. Your Father in heaven is entitled to your loyalty and love, your devotion and your allegiance. Let all creation sing praise to the Father, and let it begin with you. I worshipped the Father in every circumstance of My life on earth and I assure you that I knew hardships, tests, and physical deprivations. You, dear souls, are not the first ones to suffer during your earthly exile. Do not feel that you are in some way singled out for harsh treatment because that is not the case. Sit in the spirit of calmness and review the history of your world. It is only actually in the last century that humanity began to think that their time on earth should be devoid of suffering. People prior to this time expected suffering and they rejoiced in all that was good. They did not blame God when difficult times came. They were humble and accepting of every earthly experience. This is what I want for you. This is the approach that assures not only salvation, but happiness until you are called home. "Rejoice in our hardship?" you ask incredulously. No, My children, I do not expect you to be at a level where you can rejoice in hardship and suffering. But I would ask that you accept hardship and suffering and do not blame God. I would ask that you spread peace to all and set an example of acceptance and faith. I want this of you. I want you to tell yourself that your hardship and suffering is an opportunity to give something to God the Father and that is your loyalty and faith. Say often, "I trust You, God. I offer You my pain in the spirit of acceptance and I will serve You in every circumstance." Brothers and sisters, it is this prayer, this attitude of humble and meek acceptance that makes great saints. I will show you. Study Me as your guide. Study My life. Read about My life in Scripture and you will see My humble and meek approach to souls. Did souls scorn Me for such a countenance? No, My brothers and sisters. Good and holy souls saw that I carried heaven within Me and were drawn to Me. Good and holy souls, souls hungry for the Spirit of God, followed Me from town to town and waited for Me so that they could be close to Me. It will be the same for you. Souls will be drawn to you in their hunger because they will sense that you carry the only bread that can fill them to satisfaction. I am using you, dear ones, to

spread Me. I want to be felt in every room, every car, every place where even one soul rests in loneliness and spiritual deprivation. You will enter and I will be there. I will fill the room, the car, the place, and souls who hunger for God will feel My presence and give thanks. So do not curse hardship. Do not blame God for the pains and sorrows in this world. It is through your acceptance of these things that you will find your soul illuminated with the light of the next world.

January 21, 2004
Jesus the King

My brothers and sisters, all is well. We seek to assure you of this during this time because all does not seem well when viewed from the eyes of the world. You must allow Me to lend you My eyes. I would have you see your world from the viewpoint of your Savior, who returns to lead you into the New Time. You must follow Me in each and every moment, remaining in the present always. My children, I am giving you the antidote for grief, for fear, and for anxiety. When you remain in the present, viewing the world with My eyes and from My viewpoint, you have little to concern yourselves with aside from serving Me and allowing Me to work through you. This is the answer to the ills and darkness of your modern world. It is something that requires practice, it is true. But, like any habit, it becomes something quite easy once you are accustomed to doing it. I want each soul to know Me. I can give you this knowledge of Me if you want it but you must allow Me to do so. Say to Me often, "Jesus, what do You think of all of this? Jesus, what do You want me to do for this soul? Jesus, show me how to bring You into this situation." My brothers and sisters, you will hear My response to these queries and requests. I will not leave you guessing about what your Jesus would like. I want to explain to you that this is how it is intended that you live. This is how men of good will have been living for centuries. Men of good will live with the desire to please their God in everything. It is only in this current time that this desire is unusual and the exception. But it is My wish that we focus on the future, looking ahead to the age of obedience, which I am returning to announce. Have confidence in Me, brothers and sisters. I will not leave you in the dark without guidance. You are precious to God and important to the Kingdom. I will see that you have what you need to serve.

January 22, 2004
Jesus the King

My brothers and sisters in this suffering world, follow My example. Be brave as your Savior was brave. When you are frightened, immerse yourself in My Passion and ask yourself, "How did Jesus handle fear?" I tell you, My friends, I rested in My fears. I examined My fears closely because through that examination I discovered and reminded Myself that, truly, the fear was natural, but unnecessary. My only true fear should have been that I would fail God and lose My soul through a permanent rejection of God. You, children, have seen how I lived through Scripture and through the revelations I have made through many servants across the ages. What chance was there that I would have permanently rejected God? There was no chance of that, of course. My fears were groundless. And yet, I had to spend time with My fear and examine My fear so that I could come to that conclusion. Once I had come to the conclusion that I was going to serve God, and through that service to God save humanity, there was nothing left to fear. My future was decided. My path was lit up and I followed that path. From the time of

My arrest I felt no uncertainty. Those holy souls who witnessed My Passion would tell you that I did not rail against My fate. I did not curse God. I did not even curse humanity or My persecutors. I was the lamb. My sacrifice was perfect, both physically and mentally. Dearest brothers and sisters, whom I call as friends, you have the perfect example in Me. Follow My lead and look closely at your fears. When you have done this you will see that there is no good reason to spend time with fear and your time is much better spent consoling others, spreading My peace and Good News, and praising God, with whom you are destined to spend eternity. Every breath of praise, every sentence of praise, every song of praise you utter will surround you with an oxygen-like substance in heaven. You will breathe in all of your prayers and you will exult in every earthly acceptance of suffering or hardship. Your prayers and obedience give God glory, this is true. But your earthly prayers and obedience also give you glory in eternity. These acts of submission to your God add to the light that will surround you in heaven. You must see heaven to believe it and I cannot show you too much because you remain in service at this time. But you will never regret what you do for your brothers and sisters, what you do for the Kingdom, or what you do to bring yourself closer to Me. You understand that through these things you experience peace. That is just the beginning of your reward for these acts. You feel this peace because you are coming closer to God through these decisions on earth. Examine your fears, My friends. I will help you. And together we will toss them aside, one by one, because they do not fuel holiness, but arrest your spiritual development. As such, they must be eliminated. I am with you and it is I who wills this process of eliminating fear. It is an important goal for you.

January 23, 2004
Jesus the King

My brothers and sisters, think of Me as your dearest friend, who has been away on a journey, but who now returns. What preparation will you make for this friend? Will there not be a celebration when this friend returns? Remember that this friend has always loved you and looked out for your interests. This friend has, in fact, proved His loyalty to you by offering His life so that you could live. In short, everything this friend has, He has given to you. Now consider what preparations are appropriate. I feel that there is no preparation too good to welcome Me back to your world. I return, brothers and sisters. I am coming. Many of you will witness My return. Will you be ready to greet Me? I want this to be a joyous time for you and that is only possible with your cooperation. Prepare the Way of the Lord. Open your heart. Help Me to open the hearts of those around you. Ask Me each day, "Lord, what can I do today to prepare for Your coming? Direct me, Lord, and I will see to Your wishes." Children of God, I have explained many things to you. I have revealed many things to you. Take My words to your hearts and live by them, because, truly, My words are intended to direct you and give you comfort and consolation. My words are truth. I am Jesus. I am the King. I am returning to your world and none will deny that it is I. Some will reject Me. But you will not. You will sing praise to the Father for this merciful intervention in your world. Be with Me now as My advance cohort. Prepare for My return and you will be grateful for all eternity that you cooperated with this heavenly effort on earth. You work for Me, dear soul, and I will see to all of your interests.

January 24, 2004
God the Father

My children, you must prepare the way for Jesus. My Son returns in glory. You will see His heavenly glory illuminate the sky. Before that time, you will see His heavenly glory illuminate the souls of the just on earth. These souls will be like lightning, passing the current of divine love to other souls. Truly, in this time of transition and preparation, My loyal children have work to do. It is through you that I prepare the world. Be confident in My providence, little children, and trust your God through everything. Set the example of peaceful trust and loyal service. Will you regret that you are ready when Jesus returns? Will you regret that you assisted many souls to be ready to receive the Savior? Each soul who is ready, who welcomes Jesus, will give Him joy. The more you prepare the earth through completion of the tasks I assign to you, the greater the celebration and the greater your reward. It may be that I am asking you to serve quietly and humbly, away from all human eyes, seen only by Me. Your service is as valuable to the Kingdom as one whom I have chosen to lead multitudes. Do not put an earthly

value on your service. Only I can assign value to the tasks I have selected for you. If you are called on to serve quietly, serve quietly, united to Me in joy. If you are called on to serve loudly, serve loudly, united to Me in joy. Have My courage as I make it available to you always. You will have all that you need. When you feel you are floundering, call out to Me. I will correct any diversions in your path and renew your spirit of calm. Always thank Me for choosing you to serve. Never wish yourself somewhere else as I have chosen the exact place to use you in My Kingdom. We are together now, dear soul, so lovingly created by My divine hand, and we will be together for eternity.

Part Two:
Heaven Speaks to Priests

January 26, 2004
Jesus

My brothers in the priesthood, I direct these words to you. When I call you My brother, I do so with all love and understanding. A brother is one who has had the same general preparation for life, and as such, views life with similar vision. I am that way to you. I am your brother. You are My brother. You must view your life through eyes that see as your Savior sees. To clarify, view everything through My eyes. I am Jesus Christ. You are My divine servants. You have been given a share of My divinity through your vocation. In this way, it is not you who leads sheep back to the fold, but Me who leads through you. If you are open to Me, if you are accepting My graces, this is working. You see others respond to you and you see others led to holiness and peace. If you are not open to My graces, and My graces are not flowing through you, you see others left without divine sustenance. You have been chosen. Do not think that you have landed in your priestly vocation through a set of accidental events. This is not the case. It is not you who chose Me, My dearest son, but I who chose you. I chose you because

My Father in heaven created you to serve. You have been given gifts that I require for the coming of My Kingdom. I will bring your gifts to fruition. If you do not feel as though your gifts are good enough, or being used to the greatest advantage, it is because you are not allowing Me to infuse them with My divine Spirit. My dear brother, you must understand that My will for you incorporates all that is necessary for your priesthood to rise to the level that I intend for you. Perhaps you are struggling. Perhaps you do not feel the divine flowing through you. Please, begin anew, to walk your vocation with Me. I intend to renew you. I require your commitment to Me and to the Kingdom. In order to accomplish what I need to accomplish through you, I need you to become smaller. Ask Me with decision now to accomplish only My will through you by putting aside your own goals. My mother will help you in discerning the heavenly path. It is time to serve only heaven now, My dear brother. I will guide you and direct you in a way that will delight you if you will allow Me. If you do not spend any time considering the wonder of your vocation and the wonder of the divine in your life, it is a good sign that you need renewal. I am here. I will renew you.

January 27, 2004
Jesus

Dear sons of heaven, I call out to you now. My compassionate heart sees all that has transpired in this world and I have willed that the time of suffering and persecution for the sons of heaven is passing. You, dear ones, are the sons of heaven. You have a divine duty to maintain My holy priesthood in this world. I am no longer walking your earth in the physical sense. I do not need to, because I have you to do that for Me. You bring Me to souls, just as if I were physically present, as I was physically present to so many during My lifetime. Imagine, being called upon to be the Savior of humanity. That was My call. What is your call? Your call is to bring the Savior of humanity directly to that humanity every day. You are called upon to make the sacraments available. Dear sons of the Father, souls must repent and confess their sins. This is as I have willed. To do that, they must have priests available to administer this sacrament. Are you available to do that for God's children? If not, you must consider whether or not I am asking you to do so. The administration of the sacraments is part of your calling. Many of My sons have gone away from this priority in their lives, seeing it more as an annoyance. My sons, it is not just to serve souls that I call upon you to do these things. I also minister to you and deepen your vocation with the richest of graces during your service to souls. It is through your service to souls that you will find your salvation. Do not treat this area of your priesthood as superfluous. You must study Me and the methods I used when I walked your paths of ministry. I was always kind. I was patient. I was humble. Remember and recall that I am God. Still, I did not wield My authority as a weapon to control others. I administered My authority to others in telling the truth. I had courage, My sons. Remember and recall also that I was to be put to death for speaking the truth. Did this threat seal My lips? You know that it did not. I spoke the truth always. I feared neither the wrath of mankind nor the wrath of the enemy. Man cannot touch your soul without your permission. You would do well to remind yourself of this when you are called upon to speak a truth that will alienate others. You walk the earth during a time of challenges. Thank God for this. I intend to assist you now in every way that you can imagine. You are not alone. I walk

with you and wish to live your vocation. I can only do so with your permission and cooperation. Come back to My Sacred Heart, My dear chosen son. I have extraordinary consolations waiting for you. I want you to serve with joy and joy is possible for you in every area of your service to heaven. But you must be united to Me in order for Me to transmit this joy. I intend to infuse your soul with all wisdom and love. I wish to illuminate the truth for you so that you feel no doubt or confusion. Come to Me. Be with Me. Let Me serve you so that you may serve others.

January 28, 2004
Jesus

My brothers in service to the Father, I have such compassion for you that it swells My heart. How I understand your discouragements and fears. You toil often without the benefit of seeing the fruit of your labor. This can be difficult, but I use this absence of immediate satisfaction to increase your trust and to strengthen your faith. If you are viewing your priesthood from My eyes, you will become accustomed to seeing the vast view. Your every priestly act impacts eternity because your every priestly act impacts souls in one way or another. Do you scoff at the importance of each act? Perhaps your humility recoils at such a thought. It is not to make you self-important that I tell you this. I tell you this, My brother, to make you aware of how crucial is your service to the coming of the Kingdom. You speak with My authority. Please be aware of this. One of the difficulties of this time for you, the sons of heaven, is that many of you have inadvertently absorbed the worldly view that you have little impact on world events and souls. This is an error. This is false. This is worldly thinking and not heavenly thinking.

Think like Me, dear sons, and understand that if God is working through you, you have tremendous impact on the outcome of each life that comes in contact with your vocation. I do not want you to feel an overwhelming responsibility, but I want you to feel a responsibility. You know that I am truth. I speak only what is so and never speak falsely or with the intention of manipulation. I speak to you these truths so that you can view your vocation with the appropriate solemnity. My sons, you are heaven's treasures. I am consoled by you more than your humanity can imagine. If you understood how much consolation I took from your vocation, you might indeed feel overwhelmed with responsibility so I shield you from such a burden. I do not, however, shield you from the reality of your role in the coming of My Kingdom. Be alert during this time as I am returning. I will be working decisively through you if you allow Me. I require your cooperation for God's glory. Spend time in silence with Me, the Divine Priest.

January 29, 2004
Jesus

My brothers in service to the Father often forget that they have all of heaven to support them. You must call on this divine assistance throughout your day. In the past, priests were advised to use the heavenly counsel of their predecessors. Spend time with the warriors of God who have gone before you. They will inspire you with guidance in every imaginable situation. You are not the first one to have experienced difficulties with your vocation. I say this now with all understanding and kindness. If you have been asked to do a job you do not like, you must accept that it is I who is asking you to complete this task. I have many reasons for placing you where I have placed you and your soul and your priesthood have valuable lessons to learn. I will always see to your spiritual advancement if you see to My work in whatever capacity you are being used to serve the Kingdom. My dear soul, united to Me in the field of service to God, it is to reassure you that I come in this way. I want you to avail of all love, all guidance, and all assistance that has been put in place for your benefit and to benefit others through you. Come to heaven with every difficulty. Often My brothers forget that it is exactly what they give to others that they forget to nourish in themselves. This is the gift of faith. You must spend time alone with Me so that we can be certain that this gift is being used to its fullest advantage in your soul. I wish to do this for you, My beloved servant. If all is well with your vocation, you feel a quietness, a steadiness in service that sustains you during challenges to your faith, during restlessness, and during the inevitable frustration that is felt with any vocation. If all is not well with your vocation, you feel constrained, you are unsure, you are having difficulty transmitting faith to others because you are not certain yourself of the truths of our Church. My dear follower, if this describes you, we have work to do. Do not be afraid or think you are unsuited to follow in the footsteps of the Divine Priest. You must view these feelings as a symptom of the contagion that has spread through the world. You are living in a time that is infected by darkness. It is no surprise that some of you will also be infected. I am calm about this but I seek to remedy your spiritual illness now. You must turn it over to Me. You must be humble while I minister to you and

replace your weakness with spiritual strength. Look toward heaven. I am here. I am the light that you must walk toward. Now, at this time, do not look away. Keep your eyes focused on Me and begin your ascent. You will be given such assistance that you will clearly understand that your Savior is working and the origin of your healing is divine. My dearest, My dearest, you belong to Me. I am your God. The world is not your God. Do not worry that the darkness has pulled at you. Now I pull you back to Me. There is nothing in our way, My son, except your attachment to the world. Give it to Me. The world does not seek to love you for eternity. Only I seek such a goal. I seek your well-being. Long before I use you to serve others, I must serve you. You must allow your Jesus to minister to you now so that I can replace the beauty of your calling within you. Only then can you serve others in the manner necessary to bring about the return of the First Priest.

January 30, 2004
Jesus

I ask My brothers to renew their confidence in Me as their guide. I am your goal, always, dear souls in service. Your first priority is your unity to Me. Your relationship with Me is what should direct your vocation. In other words, if you are united to Me, you will not be questioning your actions. You will spend little time with questions about your faith, about your Church, and about how you are to respond to matters of faith in challenging situations. The reason is that all of this work is done during our prayer time, when you not only pray and praise the Godhead, but contemplate the Godhead. It is during this time that I place the answers within you and you then have ready access to the truths in your activities of service. You see, My dear brother, that many of your comrades have questions. There is a great deal of discussion about matters that require no discussion. I have given the answers through My Vicar, your Holy Father, to whom you have pledged obedience. You must stop all of the talk. It is not for you to decide these matters. It is for you to obey in these matters and set an example of joyful obedience. May I stress the word joyful here, dear one? I have given you joy in service. When you do not feel that joy, you must come back to Me, again, in prayer. We have discussed that. Your vocation should not feel like a punitive state. It should feel like the joyful liberating state that it is. You will not feel like that every day, and you should not expect to feel like that every day, because at the end of it all, love is sacrifice and your love for Me has demanded a sacrifice. Please do not think that your Jesus does not acknowledge that fact. What I want you to spend time with, though, is My love for you. My love for you has liberated you from the world long before most other souls. My love for you has brought you to a level of service in the Kingdom that ensures your eternal status. But you must serve. You will spend eternity basking in My gratitude and enjoying the Father's acknowledgement of your service on earth. I love you, My dear brother. I am filled with gratitude that you stand alongside Me and take direction from Me. Allow Me to love you. Allow Me to set your soul free from the worldly shackles that make your vocation seem like a heavy thing. I will set you free but you must pray. Make a commitment to prayer time and do not allow anything but duty to interfere. You cannot give what you do not have, and if you do not want, what you are called upon to give, your vocation will not bear fruit. I am looking into your soul at this moment. I see all. I know exactly what must be done to bring you to the fullest potential. Ask Me to do that for you. Invite Me to do that for you. And then, allow Me to do that for you. Souls are suffering all around you. You must bring Me to them. You will soon become translucent in that the brightness of My love will shine right through you and others will be warmed and strengthened, converted and confirmed by their contact with you. Do you think this is not possible? If so, then that is another sign that you must spend more time with Me. When you spend time with Me, you forget about your limitations and contemplate My infinite power. It is in this way that My infinite power can begin to flow through you, which is as it should be and as it is intended to be. Come now. You have made the commitment to serve the Kingdom. Make another commitment today to love Me. You then allow Me to love you, which gives you an overflow of love to share. This is what I need from you.

January 31, 2004
Jesus

I come back to your world in triumph, dear brothers. I come back to your world as King. What will be the reward for My faithful servants? Think for a moment in earthly terms. Consider that a king travels away from his kingdom, and during his absence many servants become unfaithful. They flaunt their disobedience and generally make a mockery of the perfect order the king had designed for the harmony of his kingdom. This results in great pain and disorder and threatens the unity of the kingdom. Because of the disarray, the kingdom is no longer fit to defend against its enemies, who gradually, and with great glee, take over the kingdom and impose their own order, which is against everything this wise and benevolent king had worked to create for his subjects. Now imagine that this enemy was neither strong, nor wise. The enemy was disorganized and had small numbers in comparison. The advantage that the enemy utilized was that most of the king's subjects had become lazy and groggy during the absence of their king. So it was with relative ease that the enemy infiltrated and overcame. But not all of the good king's subjects were asleep. There were many who remained alert, and appalled by the disorder, sought to warn their fellow subjects. These faithful ones warned that the king would return and because he was a just king, he would punish the weak ones who made decisions against the kingdom. Some listened, some did not. Either way, the faithful ones persevered and refused to be drawn into the dark celebrations of the infiltrators. They were often ridiculed for their adherence to the laws of the good king. They found that often they suffered in other ways. Many lost material advantages, some lost family relationships because of their faith, and some dear subjects gave their lives in defense of the king. Now, imagine that this good king has been consistently apprised of this state of affairs. When his journey is complete, he hastens to return to his people. Imagine his feelings upon consideration that this beautiful and harmonious kingdom he created for his people has been turned into a lawless and ugly place where his faithful servants are persecuted. I am that King. The only difference is that I have infinite power, infinite wisdom, and I read each soul with a glance. I am returning. My dear fellow priests, you are those loyal and faithful subjects who maintained the faith for Me during the time of the great disobedience. Try to imagine for a moment how I will repay your faithfulness. You decided for Me in a time when few do. You remain in My service when many have drifted off to join the din of the enemy's celebrations. You, despite the constant lure of the world, persevere to serve those loyal souls who also persevere. My heart aches with love for every soul created by My Father. This is a great truth. But I will have a divine gratitude for those who have served Me during this time of darkness. You are many, but in relation to the world, you are few. You are chosen and I will use you. I use you now. I begin to reveal your role in the process of My return. Be open to this personal directing and understand that no human living on earth can even imagine the reward I will levy upon those servants who defended the King in His absence.

February 2, 2004
Jesus

I speak with great love to My brothers in the service of the Kingdom. Dear brothers, it is you who must prepare the harvest. I return to sort the wheat from the chaff. You will help Me in so many ways. I want souls to come back to My heart now. Many souls do not feel My presence in the world because so few house the Spirit during this time. But you house My Spirit. And they will see Me in you and through your vocations and service to Me. Because, despite all of the interest in material possessions and power, the small core of the human that is the soul, longs for Me. There is nothing that can fill that divine place but the Divine Master. And if a soul does not have the Divine Master, he feels a lonely emptiness. He searches. Many search during this time and use all manner of foolishness in their attempt to fill this bitter emptiness. There is no shortage of souls who are willing to mislead My poor wandering children. But there is a shortage of souls who are willing to lead these children back to Me. I call out for more laborers. I ask that souls look at their world and then look up to heaven. Am I calling to you? Do you hear My voice in your heart, asking you to lead souls back to the light? You must listen for My voice. If you do not listen, dear child, you will never hear. Listen in silence. Ask Me to speak to you. You must ask Me to speak louder if you do not hear My voice. I will do this for you. If I am calling to you, and you are listening for My voice, all will be well. You will answer My call and I will send souls willing to assist you in finding your vocation. Young men of this troubled world, search your soul. You will find Me there and perhaps you have been created to lead in this time of transition. You need fear nothing because your Jesus will see to all. I am your beginning and your end. I am the One who seeks your eternal joy. You have been placed in this time to serve. During this time, when so many fail the Kingdom, your service is critical. You can make a decision for Me this day and you will bring many souls back to My wounded heart. You will never regret turning to Me, dear son of the Father. This is not even possible. You will only rejoice that you served. Feel My Spirit as I whisper My divine guidance into your soul. The heavenly breath of the Spirit brings peace and calm and a deep wisdom that rests in quietness. You will have all that you need. Come to Me now and I will prepare you to serve.

February 3, 2004
God the Father

My sons, My favor rests upon you. I plan for the return of My Son much as a general plots a campaign in that I gaze upon you and count you as one of My assets. You are an asset to the Kingdom of your Father. I intend to make the most possible use of your commitment to Me if you will allow Me. For Me to do that, I must have your unqualified "yes" to Me. Will you give that to your Father? I created you to serve the Kingdom during this time because I knew that your gifts would be necessary. I am going to expand your gifts by infusing them with the divine. It is I who works through you and ministers to souls. Only in this way can there be an explosion of the Holy Spirit, which is what is necessary in your world. You are preparing, but in a special way. There are those of you who might say that you have always been preparing and awaiting the return of the King. This is true, and indeed, souls have been called upon to do this for many centuries. But I tell you today that your generation will see great and terrible changes. So while I have asked My children to prepare their hearts for the coming of the King for many years, I ask you now to prepare both your hearts and the hearts of others, and also the world, for the return of the King. This is different because we are ushering in a New Time. This time will be a joyful and obedient time during which all mankind will know that I am the Creator. All mankind will know of My love for the created creature who is man. I will be justified by the rule of My Son in the world. My creatures who wish to live in harmony with Me in the world will be safe and their children will worship the one true God with confidence and peace. You are experiencing mercy at this time but this time is destined to end, like all times. The coming time will include justice and reckoning. My sons who serve in the pastures of the earthly kingdom, you must prepare souls. I have a role for you to play. It is divine and has its origin in heaven. Do not refuse Me your service when I rely so heavily on your vocation. You are Mine and all that I own will be yours. Never doubt your reward. Serve Me now in obedience and you will open a flow of the Spirit that will engulf all those around you. You must listen to My words and you must trust that they are truth. I will confirm these words in your life and you will know that I am God.

February 4, 2004
God the Father

My son, raise your eyes to Me. Let My gaze rest upon you. Do you feel the love I have for you? Do you feel My tenderness? Rest in that tenderness for a time so that I can fill you with My choicest graces. I have everything you need. You look upon your vocation and you see flaws and mistakes. I look upon your vocation and I see a servant whom I can use to minister to My poor, poor children. Can you imagine the gratitude of a Father toward a child who denies himself to save a sibling in trouble? Can you even imagine that, My son? I have that for you. That gratitude will be lavished upon you on your arrival here, but first, you must persevere for a bit longer. Do you sometimes wonder about the value of your vocation? In earthly terms, we can put no price on it. It is what is called priceless, which means that the value is so inestimable and great that no value can be assigned. Your vocation has an eternal value to My Kingdom and to our family. Your vocation is destined to change lives and to bring souls to eternity in the light, souls that otherwise would not choose the light. When you view the light, the heavenly landscape, you will understand why no value could be placed on your vocation. I love each one of My children more than the human mind can grasp. It is My will that each return to Me, to spend eternity within this family of goodness. Many are choosing darkness, My son, and that is why these words and the accompanying graces are being sent to earth. All that has occurred in your life up until this moment has prepared you. I have allowed each event so that when this time came, you would be ready. You are ready. You are prepared. You are in the place where I have put you. Look up to heaven, My dear son, and feel My love flowing down upon you. Your Savior resides within you. This Divine Priest will direct your steps. Allow Him to do that. Be like the smallest child and place your hand inside Mine now and I will lead you along the path of My service. You must practice faith, keeping nothing for yourself. All day long tell Jesus that you want Him to use you. Say this to Him:

"Jesus, how do You want to use me on this day? You have a willing servant in me, Jesus. Allow Me to work for the Kingdom."

My dear son, you are the heir to a great fortune. Do not reject your inheritance for

a world that does not recognize your worth. Serve your Father in humility and you will experience the true joy that is your vocation.

February 5, 2004
God the Father

My sons, you are true men of heaven and all of heaven understands your struggle and supports you through intercessory powers. If you are having a difficult time, you must take advantage of this kinship and appeal to those who have gone before you. My family is very large, but My family works much like the best Christian family on earth in that we all assist each other. We have the divine vision in heaven so those souls joined with Me here can see your mission and they understand what is necessary for the most successful outcome of your work. My dear servants, it is for this reason that they are the better judges of what will help you than the wisest earthly counsel. Utilize this system of brother helping brother and sister helping sister. "How do we do that, God?" you ask. I will tell you. You must first of all understand that your struggles have been vanquished by others before you. There is nothing new in that sense. The sons and daughters of the light have always had to battle the powers of darkness who do not like to see true servants completing their duties. That is not new. You live in a remarkable time in that Jesus is returning and the process has begun. You have been called upon to help usher in that New Time. This is different but your duties are the same duties that your brothers and sisters have had to accomplish before you. So you experience complete understanding from heaven. Learn about the struggles of these triumphant souls. Study their lives and see how they dealt with temptation and evil. Most of what you will learn is quite simple in that these souls rose every day and did their duty according to their vocations. This is what you must do. But it is very consoling for those of you still in exile to see that your struggles have been seen before and that My sustaining hand steadied others when they were fearful or uncertain. I am with you. I send all manner of heavenly assistance. You must not think that your vocation can survive by your own power. Your vocation will not thrive unless you understand that it is I who fuels your soul and I who touches others. You are the instrument whom I use to serve others but the grace originates with Me in heaven. There are many who have difficulty because this age of disobedience fosters great human arrogance. Search your soul and root this out. Humility will open your soul, dear son. Humility is the understanding that

without Me you are earthbound in your thinking, like those souls who have rejected Me. Do you want that? Can you commit to a life where you do not have Me to sustain and direct you? If the answer is no, and of course it must be, then you must come fully over to the other side and understand that I am God, and you are My servant.

February 6, 2004
God the Father

Sons of heaven, listen to My voice. You hear with your ears, now you must listen with your hearts. All that is noble about mankind is possible for you, but not without unity to My Son. Unite yourself to the Divine Priest and all will become easy for you. Through this unity you will develop into the highest possible version of a heavenly servant who remains on earth. You must want this and you must work for this, but you cannot grasp it in the way of most earthly acquisitions. To grasp this possession of holiness, you must relinquish your grasp on the world. You must give your attachments to the world to Me. Lay them at My feet, dear son, destined to be held against Me in love. Lay these attachments at My feet and I will eradicate their hold on you. This may be difficult at first but soon it will become a habit and you will have escaped this snare. Do not be discouraged if you find you must lay these attachments at My feet every morning. So be it. Do I tire of helping you? Of course I do not. I created you and you responded to My dominion over you by accepting the gift of your vocation. Now I want you to accept the gift of your mission. We must strengthen you in every spiritual way. Again, the way to become strong in this service is to become weak and allow My strength, and the strength of all of My Kingdom, to flow through you. I anticipate your mistakes and forgive them. I anticipate your successes and celebrate them. I prepare your reward. Serve, My son. Serve.

Part Three:
Jesus Speaks to Sinners

February 16, 2004
Jesus

Listen to My voice as I call to you. Dear soul, entangled in the darkness of this world, it is to you I cry out. I am your Savior. I am calling to you loudly now because the time for you to hear My voice has arrived. No longer should you turn away from Me. Dear soul of the Kingdom, you belong with your family. Who is your family, you ask. We are your family. You have a great many souls here on earth who will love you but you must come back to Christianity. Christianity is simply the following of Christ. And who is this Christ? I am this Christ. I am Jesus, who died on the cross for you. My sacrifice made it possible for you to enjoy heaven. Let Me tell you about Me, so you will understand who loves you, and who it is you are being called to follow. I walked your earth as you do. I saw the failings of mankind as you see them. I was grieved at the injustices, in the same way that you are grieved when you see things that are not fair. Did I grow bitter? No. I did not. Why was that? Because I am God? No. I was God on earth but I was God trapped in man's body and constrained by the limitations of the body. I did this so that when it came time for you to follow Me you could not say that it was easy for Me because I was God. I did not use My divinity except during the last three years and then only to heal, cure, and otherwise support My claim that I was the King of Heaven, come down to lead all back to the Father. I did not waste miracles on those who would reject Me, regardless of proof of My divinity. Do you intend to reject Me? You are Mine, dearest soul. Come back to Me that I may introduce you to love and joy. I want to tell you why I did not grow bitter on earth. I did not grow bitter because I knew that many would follow Me. And I did not grow bitter because I knew that you would return to Me. Can you believe that you are that important to Me? I assure you, it is true. At this moment, there is only you and I. I am looking at you now. Will you return My gaze, you poor child whose heart is frozen? My love pours out upon you. My graces flow down to you. Open your heart, dear soul. Ask Me to come to you. I am here. I am waiting to love you. Do not freeze Me out any longer. Everything is possible for Me. I can heal you and cure you in an instant if you will let Me. Ask Me, dear child. You are part of My family and My family aches to have you back. I am calling you by name. Close your eyes

and listen to My voice. I am asking that you say simply, "Jesus, love me." I will take care of everything else. You feel My presence now and you can rest in My love as I transform your heart. No fear, dear child. All is well when God is present, and truly, I am with you.

February 17, 2004
Jesus

My children, I call you My children because you were created by Me. I am your God. I am the only God. Believe Me when I say to you that you will never have peace, true peace, while you are separated from Me. And your eternity must be considered. You will spend eternity in one of two places, dear little soul. You must give this serious thought and determine where you would like to reside. You say you do not believe in God or you do not believe that God would send people to hell forever. I tell you today that it is not I, the only God there is, who condemns souls to hell. It is the soul himself who chooses to reside in hell. Do you know why the soul chooses hell? Because there are like-minded souls there. A soul who aligns himself with darkness does not choose heaven because that soul would not be comfortable in heaven. You must understand that you can be angry with God but God is not at fault. You can blame God for all that is wrong with your world and perhaps this will work for you on earth. I assure you, though, on this day that this will cease to work for you at the moment of your death. At that time there will be only yourself to blame as the truth is inescapable. You will be facing the one, the only, and the true God and attempting to tell Him that He does not exist. How do you think this will go for you? It will not go well, dear soul, and that is why I am speaking to you now. I want you to divert from this path that leads to damnation. You are choosing against Me now and I am asking you to stop. I love you. There are many Christians in this world who love you and My love will flow through them to you. I want you for My Kingdom. I need you to serve Me. You are capable of the highest goodness. You are capable of bringing many souls to heaven for Me. Some of My greatest friends were far worse sinners than you. Please come back to Me. I love you and I can heal you and cure you. My forgiveness is yours. That hardly needs to be said. The greater difficulty will be in persuading you to forgive yourself but I am God and that would be only a small miracle for Me to perform. I will do that for you. I will make of you another Jesus, walking the earth in love. Do you want this? Can you picture it? Now, do not wait any longer. I shower you with graces. Lift your precious face to the heavens and feel My love as I beseech you to turn away from sin and follow Me.

February 18, 2004
Jesus

Dear souls, I have come to lead you out of darkness. When a soul remains in darkness for a long period of time, the soul becomes accustomed to the absence of light. This soul then fails to understand on a daily basis that he dwells in a Godless void. In arrogance a soul might say, "I'm quite happy without your God and do not wish to know Him." Because I am God, I know everything. I know that you are in distress. I know that your soul is immersed in bitterness, despite objections you make to support your arrogance. Dear soul, I want you to look at Me. You do not offend Me by your demand for proof. I have dealt with far more belligerent souls than you. Ask Me to speak to you in your heart. I will do so. You want to know that I exist? I will show you that I exist. Will you then follow Me? I challenge you to make that commitment to Me. If I speak to you in your soul and you hear My voice, will you then forsake darkness and return to My fold? You find your courage failing you, dear soul. You must be braver than this if you are going to be a servant of Christ. I am here. I am watching your every step and hearing

your every word. I want you back. I wish to draw you against My heart and keep you there for all of eternity. I want to hear your joyful laughter again and I want to heal every wound that has been inflicted on you by others who should have loved you. I can do that. You look for answers. You look for consolations. Do you realize how many times a day you walk past Me? Have you any idea how I stand watching you in every situation and observe your pain? You ridicule Me, dear child of God. I hear you. I am offended by you and yet I never leave you and never stop hoping that you will look at Me. If you close your eyes now and look for Me, I will come to you.

February 19, 2004
Jesus

My souls, I call you My souls because it is I who created you. You would like to object to this and say that you were created through a series of biological events. You would like to explain Me away. Dear souls, it is I who ordained the biological event that was your birth. As I ordained it, I could have cancelled it. I could have easily said, "No, this soul will not serve Me as I would like to be served, therefore I will cancel his birth." Why did I not do that? What prevented Me from interrupting the birth of a soul destined to rebel against Me, setting a bad example for others? I tell you solemnly on this day that I rejoiced at your birth because I loved you. I do not stop loving a soul when he hurts Me. Does a parent stop loving their small child when the small child disobeys? The child grows older and continues to disobey. Can the parent ever truly stop loving their child? In most cases, no. A parent continues to love the child, always hoping the child will one day return their love. I am the same with you. I do exist, dear one and your saying that I do not exist does not alter that fact. Here I am. I am speaking to you. I am knocking on the door of your heart once again. Will you answer Me today? Will you allow Me into your heart? I have such work to do there, My little wounded one. I look at you and see exactly what you are capable of becoming. Do you think it is also a biological event that you hold these words in your hand and read them? My little soul, so destined to be loved by Me, allow your soul to lead you for a moment and believe that I want you back in My heart. There is a place here for you and without you, I am alone. I love you as though you were My only child. There is just you and I at this moment. I do not want you to be lost. There is work in My Kingdom for you and this work can only be done by you. Please serve, dearest, so that we can begin travelling together. I am waiting for you. I forgive you everything. Come back to Me and you will understand freedom and joy.

February 20, 2004
Jesus

Dear children of God, why do you persist in living outside of My light? Do you think I want to harm you in some way? Do you think it will be more difficult to live your life if you follow Me and live as I have ordained? I want you to look closely today at your life, at your relationships, and at your level of contentment. Do you have true peace? Are others drawn to you because love flows from you? Do you communicate joy to others? That is what I offer. You should possess true peace and security and joy and love should flow from you. Not a false peace, offered by the world and those that avoid Me. That peace does not last and does not pierce the boundary of your soul. The temporary peace offered by the world numbs your pain for a time, leading you to believe you have found the object of your search. Then that feeling wears off and you begin to search again, always looking for that thing which can only be found in Me. Shall I minister to you? Would you like Me to infuse your soul with courage and joy? Dear one, that is what I do for My true followers. They do not escape life's difficulties. They have a steadiness that sets them apart from those who do not follow Me and who do not take advantage of heaven's gifts. I want to share these gifts. On this day I want you to tell Me all day long that you believe in Me. You may not feel this. You may have a difficult time even forming the words. But in your heart, all of this day, tell Me this. I can then give you graces that will help your disbelief. We will begin to shift the stubborn doubts sowed by the father of lies. You have nothing to lose. You have tried many other remedies for your discontent. Some of you have abused your bodies in an attempt to quiet the cries of your soul. I want you to think of Me as another remedy for any difficult symptoms you are experiencing. If I do not keep My promise, to grant you peace and joy, then you may continue your search. But you must give Me a chance and to do that you must spend time in silence with Me. Come to a church that houses a tabernacle. Sit before Me in silence. Allow Me to speak to you and I will speak to you. Be brave, little soul. You have tried many more daring things than this, have you not? Come to Me now and give your God a chance.

February 21, 2004
Jesus

My children in darkness turn away from Me and from anything that reminds them of Me. Why do you look away when you see something that reminds you of Me? What is it inside you that causes this feeling of restlessness or anxiety? Is it because when your eyes rest upon something that reminds you of holiness you fear that you are not holy? Consider for a moment that it is the remnant of your conscience that is telling you to pay attention. You pull away because you know that if you pay attention you will have to change. The word change implies something new, but it also implies abandoning something old. In your case, you would be abandoning sin, which has not made you happy. Dear soul, destined for heaven, do not turn quickly away when your eyes rest upon an image of Me or of one of My servants. Force yourself to hold the gaze of the Holy One. I am indeed returning your look. You sense this or you would not turn away in discomfort. I fear you misread the look that you see in My eyes. My eyes are not condemning you. I understand more than you yourself understand about why you walked down the path of darkness. You will never need to explain anything to Me. I do encourage you to converse with Me but it is for your clarity and not Mine. Is there someone in your life whose wisdom you often seek? You go to that person for advice or counsel because you trust that person's judgment. As wise as that person may be, that person's wisdom is nothing in comparison to My wisdom and I have the added asset of a complete and total love for you. I care about every detail of your life. I know you better than you know yourself and My motives are completely pure. I want what is best for you and only what is best for you. I do not seek to exploit you as the world does. You can trust Me, dear soul. Please talk to Me. Then, in turn, you will listen to Me. Then we will become friends and you will understand that no friendship on earth is as secure as the friendship between you and I. I will give you everything. What will you give Me? You will give Me your love. You will give Me your loyalty. You will give Me your willingness to change, dearest, and that is what I want from you. It is difficult perhaps at first to envision a new way to awaken and proceed into each day but you can begin slowly. Each morning, when you awaken, say, "Jesus, I give You my day." That is all. Begin there and you will see change immediately. I need only your willingness. All will flow from there. You must be brave but I will give you courage. It all comes from Me.

February 22, 2004
Jesus

I am with you, dear sinners. It is for you I came the first time and it is for you I return. My mercy knows no limits and this limitless mercy is being poured out upon your world. Let it flow through you. You must also encourage others to come back to Me. That is your mission. I want you to be reconciled with Me. I want you to feel My peace and then extend My peace to others. You will know My joy, dear soul. And then you will spread My joy. Receive these words as the great gift they are and welcome them for what they will bring to you. They will bring you heaven if you allow them to work in your soul. I have only positive designs on you. Your time here on earth, when you are temporarily exiled from heaven, is the time for you to serve the Kingdom of God. This Kingdom is incomplete without your service and souls whom you are destined to bring to Me might be left. I compensate for the failures of My children on earth, of course, or too many would be left unloved during this time, but I need your service. When the end of earthly time comes, far into the future, then all will be complete, and completed in heaven. For now, we must struggle, we must grow in size, and we must persevere. I love you. I have forgiven you everything you have ever done against Me or against yourself. You are welcome in My arms and there is a place in My heart for you. If you make the smallest movement toward Me, you will see Me act with great speed to pull you back into the safety of your Christian family. My child, will you answer your Jesus? It is My voice you hear calling out your name. Come to Me now. You will look back on your life someday and you will see this moment as very important for your eternity. Do not hesitate. Your time is over and Mine has begun. Fear nothing. Accept My joy and accept My light. In all quietness, turn your eyes to Mine.

Appendix

The Lay Apostolate of Jesus Christ the Returning King

We seek to be united to Jesus in our daily work, and through our vocations, in order to obtain graces for the conversion of sinners. Through our cooperation with the Holy Spirit, we will allow Jesus to flow through us to the world, bringing His light. We do this in union with Mary, our Blessed Mother, with the Communion of Saints, with all of God's holy angels, and with our fellow lay apostles in the world.

Guidelines for Lay Apostles

As lay apostles of Jesus Christ the Returning King, we agree to perform our basic obligations as practicing Catholics. Additionally, we will adopt the following spiritual practices, as best we can:

1. **Allegiance Prayer** and **Morning Offering**, plus a brief prayer for the Holy Father
2. **Eucharistic Adoration**, one hour per week
3. **Prayer Group Participation**, monthly, at which we pray the Luminous Mysteries of the Holy Rosary and read the Monthly Message
4. **Monthly Confession**
5. Further, we will follow the example of Jesus Christ as set out in the Holy Scripture, treating all others with His patience and kindness.

Allegiance Prayer

Dear God in Heaven, I pledge my allegiance to You. I give You my life, my work and my heart. In turn, give me the grace of obeying Your every direction to the fullest possible extent. Amen.

Morning Offering

O Jesus, through the Immaculate Heart of Mary, I offer You the prayers, works, joys and sufferings of this day, for all the intentions of Your Sacred Heart, in union with the Holy Sacrifice of the Mass throughout the world, in reparation for my sins, and for the intentions of the Holy Father. Amen.

Prayer for the Holy Father

Blessed Mary, Mother of Jesus, protect our Holy Father, Benedict XVI, and bless his intentions.

Five Luminous Mysteries

1. The Baptism of Jesus
2. The Wedding at Cana
3. The Proclamation of the Kingdom of God
4. The Transfiguration
5. The Institution of the Eucharist

Promise from Jesus to His Lay Apostles

May 12, 2005

Your message to souls remains constant. Welcome each soul to the rescue mission. You may assure each lay apostle that just as they concern themselves with My interests, I will concern Myself with theirs. They will be placed in My Sacred Heart and I will defend and protect them. I will also pursue complete conversion of each of their loved ones. So you see, the souls who serve in this rescue mission as My beloved lay apostles will know peace. The world cannot make this promise as only Heaven can bestow peace on a soul. This is truly Heaven's mission and I call every one of Heaven's children to assist Me. You will be well rewarded, My dear ones.

Prayers taken from The Volumes

Prayers to God the Father

"What can I do for my Father in Heaven?"

"I trust You, God. I offer You my pain in the spirit of acceptance and I will serve You in every circumstance."

"God my Father in Heaven, You are all mercy. You love me and see my every sin. God, I call on You now as the Merciful Father. Forgive my every sin. Wash away the stains on my soul so that I may once again rest in complete innocence. I trust You, Father in Heaven. I rely on You. I thank You. Amen."

"God my Father, calm my spirit and direct my path."

"God, I have made mistakes. I am sorry. I am Your child, though, and seek to be united to You."

"I believe in God. I believe Jesus is calling me. I believe my Blessed Mother has requested my help. Therefore I am going to pray on this day and every day."

"God my Father, help me to understand."

Prayers to Jesus

"Jesus, I give You my day."

"Jesus, how do You want to use me on this day? You have a willing servant in me, Jesus. Allow me to work for the Kingdom."

"Lord, what can I do today to prepare for Your coming? Direct me, Lord, and I will see to Your wishes."

"Lord, help me."

"Jesus, love me."

Prayers to the Angels

"Angels from Heaven, direct my path."

"Dearest angel guardian, I desire to serve Jesus by remaining at peace. Please obtain for me the graces necessary to maintain His divine peace in my heart."

Prayers for a Struggling Soul

"Jesus, what do You think of all this? Jesus, what do You want me to do for this soul? Jesus, show me how to bring You into this situation."

"Angel guardian, thank you for your constant vigil over this soul. Saints in Heaven, please assist this dear angel."

Prayers for Children

"God in Heaven, You are the Creator of all things. Please send Your graces down upon our world."

"Jesus, I love You."

"Jesus, I trust in You. Jesus, I trust in You. Jesus, I trust in You."

"Jesus, I offer You my day."

"Mother Mary, help me to be good."

How to Recite the Chaplet of Divine Mercy

The Chaplet of Mercy is recited using ordinary Rosary beads of five decades. The Chaplet is preceded by two opening prayers from the *Diary* of Saint Faustina and followed by a closing prayer.

1. Make the Sign of the Cross

In the name of the Father, and of the Son, and of the Holy Spirit. Amen.

2. Optional Opening Prayers

You expired, Jesus, but the source of life gushed forth for souls, and the ocean of mercy opened up for the whole world. O Fount of Life, unfathomable Divine Mercy, envelop the whole world and empty Yourself out upon us.

O Blood and Water, which gushed forth from the Heart of Jesus as a fountain of mercy for us, I trust in You!

3. Our Father

Our Father, who art in Heaven, hallowed be Thy name. Thy Kingdom come. Thy will be done on earth as it is in Heaven. Give us this day our daily bread. And forgive us our trespasses, as we forgive those who trespass against us. And lead us not into temptation, but deliver us from evil. Amen.

4. Hail Mary

Hail Mary, full of grace, the Lord is with thee. Blessed art thou among women, and blessed is the fruit of thy womb, Jesus. Holy Mary, Mother of God, pray for us sinners, now and at the hour of our death. Amen.

5. The Apostles' Creed

I believe in God, the Father Almighty, Creator of Heaven and earth. I believe in Jesus Christ, His only Son, our Lord. He was conceived by the power of the Holy Spirit and born of the Virgin Mary. He suffered under Pontius Pilate, was crucified, died, and was buried. He descended to the dead. On the third day He rose again. He ascended into Heaven, and is seated at the right hand of the Father. He will come again to judge the living and the dead. I believe in the Holy Spirit, the holy Catholic Church, the Communion of Saints, the forgiveness of sins, the resurrection of the body, and life everlasting. Amen.

6. The Eternal Father

Eternal Father, I offer You the Body and Blood, Soul and Divinity of Your dearly beloved Son, our Lord, Jesus Christ, in atonement for our sins and those of the whole world.

7. On the Ten Small Beads of Each Decade

For the sake of His Sorrowful Passion, have mercy on us and on the whole world.

8. Repeat for the remaining decades

Saying the "Eternal Father" (6) on the "Our Father" bead and then 10 "For the sake of His Sorrowful Passion" (7) on the following "Hail Mary" beads.

9. Conclude with Holy God

Holy God, Holy Mighty One, Holy Immortal One, have mercy on us and on the whole world.

10. Optional Closing Prayer

Eternal God, in whom mercy is endless and the treasury of compassion inexhaustible, look kindly upon us and increase Your mercy in us, that in difficult moments we might not despair nor become despondent, but with great confidence submit ourselves to Your holy will, which is Love and Mercy itself.

To learn more about the image of The Divine Mercy, the Chaplet of Divine Mercy and the series of revelations given to St. Faustina Kowalska please contact:

Marians of the Immaculate Conception
Stockbridge, Massachusetts 01263
Telephone 800-462-7426
www.marian.org

How to Pray the Rosary

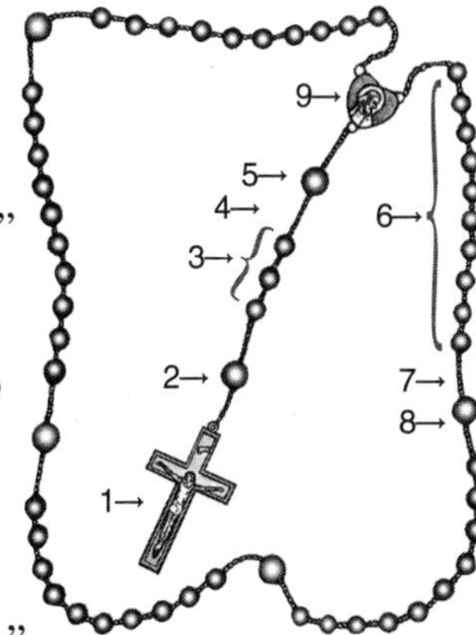

1. Make the Sign of the Cross and say the "Apostles Creed."
2. Say the "Our Father."
3. Say three "Hail Marys."
4. Say the "Glory be to the Father."
5. Announce the First Mystery; then say the "Our Father."
6. Say ten "Hail Marys," while meditating on the Mystery.
7. Say the "Glory be to the Father." After each decade say the following prayer requested by the Blessed Virgin Mary at Fatima: "O my Jesus, forgive us our sins, save us from the fires of hell, lead all souls to Heaven, especially those in most need of Thy mercy."
8. Announce the Second Mystery: then say the "Our Father." Repeat 6 and 7 and continue with the Third, Fourth, and Fifth Mysteries in the same manner.
9. Say the "Hail, Holy Queen" on the medal after the five decades are completed.

As a general rule, depending on the season, the Joyful Mysteries are said on Monday and Saturday; the Sorrowful Mysteries on Tuesday and Friday;

the Glorious Mysteries on Wednesday and Sunday; and the Luminous Mysteries on Thursday.

Papal Reflections of the Mysteries

The Joyful Mysteries

The Joyful Mysteries are marked by the joy radiating from the event of the Incarnation. This is clear from the very first mystery, the Annunciation, where Gabriel's greeting to the Virgin of Nazareth is linked to an invitation to messianic joy: "Rejoice, Mary." The whole of salvation… had led up to this greeting. (Prayed on Mondays and Saturdays, and optional on Sundays during Advent and the Christmas Season.)

The Luminous Mysteries

Moving on from the infancy and the hidden life in Nazareth to the public life of Jesus, our contemplation brings us to those mysteries which may be called in a special way "Mysteries of Light." Certainly, the whole mystery of Christ is a mystery of light. He is the "Light of the world" (John 8:12). Yet this truth emerges in a special way during the years of His public life. (Prayed on Thursdays.)

The Sorrowful Mysteries

The Gospels give great prominence to the Sorrowful Mysteries of Christ. From the beginning, Christian piety, especially during the Lenten devotion of the Way of the Cross, has focused on the individual moments of the Passion, realizing that here is found the culmination of the revelation of God's love and the source of our salvation. (Prayed on Tuesdays and Fridays, and optional on Sundays during Lent.)

The Glorious Mysteries

"The contemplation of Christ's face cannot stop at the image of the Crucified One. He is the Risen One!" The Rosary has always expressed this knowledge born of faith and invited the believer to pass beyond the darkness of the Passion in order to gaze upon Christ's glory in the Resurrection and Ascension… Mary herself would be raised to that same glory in the Assumption. (Prayed on Wednesdays and Sundays.)

From the *Apostolic Letter The Rosary of the Virgin Mary*, Pope John Paul II, Oct. 16, 2002.

Prayers of the Rosary

The Sign of the Cross

In the name of the Father, and of the Son, and of the Holy Spirit. Amen.

The Apostles' Creed

I believe in God, the Father Almighty, Creator of Heaven and earth. I believe in Jesus Christ, His only Son, our Lord. He was conceived by the power of the Holy Spirit and born of the Virgin Mary. He suffered under Pontius Pilate, was crucified, died, and was buried. He descended to the dead. On the third day He rose again. He ascended into Heaven, and is seated at the right hand of the Father. He will come again to judge the living and the dead. I believe in the Holy Spirit, the holy Catholic Church, the Communion of Saints, the forgiveness of sins, the resurrection of the body, and life everlasting. Amen.

Our Father

Our Father, who art in Heaven, hallowed be Thy name. Thy Kingdom come. Thy will be done on earth as it is in Heaven. Give us this day our daily bread. And forgive us our trespasses, as we forgive those who trespass against us. And lead us not into temptation, but deliver us from evil. Amen.

Hail Mary

Hail Mary, full of grace, the Lord is with thee. Blessed art thou among women, and blessed is the fruit of thy womb, Jesus. Holy Mary, Mother of God, pray for us sinners, now and at the hour of our death. Amen.

Glory Be to the Father

Glory be to the Father, and to the Son, and to the Holy Spirit. As it was in the beginning, is now, and ever shall be, world without end. Amen.

Hail Holy Queen

Hail, Holy Queen, Mother of Mercy, our life, our sweetness and our hope. To thee do we cry, poor banished children of Eve. To thee do we send up our sighs, mourning and weeping in this valley of tears. Turn then, most gracious Advocate, thine eyes of mercy towards us. And after this, our exile, show unto us the blessed fruit of thy womb, Jesus. O clement, O loving, O sweet Virgin Mary!

Pray for us, O Holy Mother of God.
That we may be made worthy of the promises of Christ.

The Mysteries

First Joyful Mystery: The Annunciation

And when the angel had come to her, he said, "Hail, full of grace, the Lord is with thee. Blessed art thou among women." (*Luke* 1:28)

One *Our Father*, Ten *Hail Marys*,
One *Glory Be*, etc.

Fruit of the Mystery: ***Humility***

Second Joyful Mystery: The Visitation

Elizabeth was filled with the Holy Spirit and cried out in a loud voice: "Blest are you among women and blest is the fruit of your womb."(*Luke* 1:41-42)

One *Our Father*, Ten *Hail Marys*,
One *Glory Be*, etc.

Fruit of the Mystery: ***Love of Neighbor***

Third Joyful Mystery: The Birth of Jesus

She gave birth to her first-born Son and wrapped Him in swaddling clothes and laid Him in a manger, because there was no room for them in the place where travelers lodged. (*Luke* 2:7)

One *Our Father*, Ten *Hail Marys*,
One *Glory Be*, etc.

Fruit of the Mystery: ***Poverty***

Fourth Joyful Mystery: The Presentation

When the day came to purify them according to the law of Moses, the couple brought Him up to Jerusalem so that He could be presented to the Lord, for it is written in the law of the Lord, "Every first-born male shall be consecrated to the Lord."

(*Luke* 2:22-23)

One *Our Father*, Ten *Hail Marys*,
One *Glory Be*, etc.

Fruit of the Mystery: ***Obedience***

Fifth Joyful Mystery: The Finding of the Child Jesus in the Temple

On the third day they came upon Him in the temple sitting in the midst of the teachers, listening to them and asking them questions. (*Luke* 2:46)

One *Our Father*, Ten *Hail Marys*,
One *Glory Be*, etc.

Fruit of the Mystery: ***Joy in Finding Jesus***

First Luminous Mystery: The Baptism of Jesus

And when Jesus was baptized… the heavens were opened and He saw the Spirit of God descending like a dove, and alighting on Him, and lo, a voice from heaven, saying "this is My beloved Son," with whom I am well pleased." (*Matthew* 3:16-17)

One *Our Father*, Ten *Hail Marys*,
One *Glory Be*, etc.

Fruit of the Mystery: ***Openness to the Holy Spirit***

Second Luminous Mystery: The Wedding at Cana

His mother said to the servants, “Do whatever He tells you.”… Jesus said to them, “Fill the jars with water.” And they filled them up to the brim.

(*John* 2:5-7)

One *Our Father*, Ten *Hail Marys*,
One *Glory Be*, etc.

Fruit of the Mystery: ***To Jesus through Mary***

Third Luminous Mystery: The Proclamation of the Kingdom of God

“And preach as you go, saying, ‘The kingdom of heaven is at hand.’ Heal the sick, raise the dead, cleanse lepers, cast out demons. You received without pay, give without pay.” (*Matthew* 10:7-8)

One *Our Father*, Ten *Hail Marys*,
One *Glory Be*, etc.

Fruit of the Mystery: ***Repentance and Trust in God***

Fourth Luminous Mystery: The Transfiguration

And as He was praying, the appearance of His countenance was altered and His raiment become dazzling white. And a voice came out of the cloud saying, “This is My Son, My chosen; listen to Him!

(*Luke* 9:29, 35)

One *Our Father*, Ten *Hail Marys*,
One *Glory Be*, etc.

Fruit of the Mystery: ***Desire for Holiness***

Fifth Luminous Mystery: The Institution of the Eucharist

And He took bread, and when He had given thanks He broke it and gave it to them, saying, "This is My body which is given for you."… And likewise the cup after supper, saying, "This cup which is poured out for you is the new covenant in My blood."

(*Luke* 22:19-20)

One *Our Father*, Ten *Hail Marys*,
One *Glory Be*, etc.

Fruit of the Mystery: ***Adoration***

First Sorrowful Mystery: The Agony in the Garden

In His anguish He prayed with all the greater intensity, and His sweat became like drops of blood falling to the ground. Then He rose from prayer and came to His disciples, only to find them asleep, exhausted with grief. (*Luke* 22:44-45)

One *Our Father*, Ten *Hail Marys*,
One *Glory Be*, etc.

Fruit of the Mystery: ***Sorrow for Sin***

Second Sorrowful Mystery: The Scourging at the Pillar

Pilate's next move was to take Jesus and have Him scourged. (*John* 19:1)

One *Our Father*, Ten *Hail Marys*,
One *Glory Be*, etc.

Fruit of the Mystery: ***Purity***

Third Sorrowful Mystery: The Crowning with Thorns

They stripped off His clothes and wrapped Him in a scarlet military cloak. Weaving a crown out of thorns they fixed it on His head, and stuck a reed in His right hand… (*Matthew* 27:28-29)

One *Our Father*, Ten *Hail Marys*,
One *Glory Be*, etc.

Fruit of the Mystery: ***Courage***

Fourth Sorrowful Mystery: The Carrying of the Cross

… carrying the cross by Himself, He went out to what is called the Place of the Skull (in Hebrew, Golgotha). (*John* 19:17)

One *Our Father*, Ten *Hail Marys*,
One *Glory Be*, etc.

Fruit of the Mystery: ***Patience***

Fifth Sorrowful Mystery: The Crucifixion

Jesus uttered a loud cry and said, "Father, into Your hands I commend My spirit." After He said this, He expired. (*Luke* 23:46)

One *Our Father*, Ten *Hail Marys*,
One *Glory Be*, etc.

Fruit of the Mystery: ***Perseverance***

First Glorious Mystery: The Resurrection

You need not be amazed! You are looking for Jesus of Nazareth, the one who was crucified. He has been raised up; He is not here. See the place where they laid Him." (*Mark* 16:6)

One *Our Father*, Ten *Hail Marys*,
One *Glory Be*, etc.

Fruit of the Mystery: ***Faith***

Second Glorious Mystery: The Ascension

Then, after speaking to them, the Lord Jesus was taken up into Heaven and took His seat at God's right hand. (*Mark* 16:19)

One *Our Father*, Ten *Hail Marys*,
One *Glory Be*, etc.

Fruit of the Mystery: ***Hope***

Third Glorious Mystery: The Descent of the Holy Spirit

All were filled with the Holy Spirit. They began to express themselves in foreign tongues and make bold proclamation as the Spirit prompted them. (*Acts* 2:4)

One *Our Father*, Ten *Hail Marys*,
One *Glory Be*, etc.

Fruit of the Mystery: ***Love of God***

Fourth Glorious Mystery: The Assumption

You are the glory of Jerusalem... you are the splendid boast of our people... God is pleased with what you have wrought. May you be blessed by the Lord Almighty forever and ever.

(*Judith* 15:9-10)

One *Our Father*, Ten *Hail Marys*,
One *Glory Be*, etc.

Fruit of the Mystery: ***Grace of a Happy Death***

Fifth Glorious Mystery: The Coronation

A great sign appeared in the sky, a woman clothed with the sun, with the moon under her feet, and on her head a crown of twelve stars. (*Revelation* 12:1)

One *Our Father*, Ten *Hail Marys*,
One *Glory Be*, etc.

Fruit of the Mystery: ***Trust in Mary's Intercession***

This book is part of a non-profit mission.
Our Lord has requested that we
spread these words internationally.

Please help us.

If you would like to assist us financially,
please send your tax-deductible contribution
to the address below:

Direction for Our Times
9000 West 81st Street
Justice, Illinois 60458

708-496-9300
contactus@directionforourtimes.com

www.directionforourtimes.org

Direction for Our Times Ireland
The Hague Building
Cullies
Cavan
County Cavan
Ireland

+353-(0)49-437-3040

E-mail: Contactus@dfot.ie

Direction for Our Times is a 501(c)(3)
non-profit corporation. Contributions are
deductible to the extent provided by law.

The Volumes

Direction for Our Times
as given to Anne, a lay apostle

Volume One:	***Thoughts on Spirituality***
Volume Two:	***Conversations with the Eucharistic Heart of Jesus***
Volume Three:	***God the Father Speaks to His Children*** ***The Blessed Mother Speaks to Her Bishops and Priests***
Volume Four:	***Jesus the King*** ***Heaven Speaks to Priests*** ***Jesus Speaks to Sinners***
Volume Six:	***Heaven Speaks to Families***
Volume Seven:	***Greetings from Heaven***
Volume Nine:	***Angels***
Volume Ten:	***Jesus Speaks to His Apostles***

Volumes Five and Eight will be printed at a later date.

The Volumes are now available in PDF format for free download and printing from our website: www.directionforourtimes.org. We encourage everyone to print and distribute them.

The Volumes are also available at your local bookstore.

The "Heaven Speaks" Booklets

Direction for Our Times
as given to Anne, a lay apostle

The following booklets are available individually from Direction for Our Times:

Heaven Speaks About Abortion
Heaven Speaks About Addictions
Heaven Speaks to Victims of Clerical Abuse
Heaven Speaks to Consecrated Souls
Heaven Speaks About Depression
Heaven Speaks About Divorce
Heaven Speaks to Prisoners
Heaven Speaks to Soldiers
Heaven Speaks About Stress
Heaven Speaks to Young Adults

Heaven Speaks to Those Away from the Church
Heaven Speaks to Those Considering Suicide
Heaven Speaks to Those Who Do Not Know Jesus
Heaven Speaks to Those Who Are Dying
Heaven Speaks to Those Who Experience Tragedy
Heaven Speaks to Those Who Fear Purgatory
Heaven Speaks to Those Who Have Rejected God
Heaven Speaks to Those Who Struggle to Forgive
Heaven Speaks to Those Who Suffer from Financial Need
Heaven Speaks to Parents Who Worry About Their Children's Salvation

All twenty of the "Heaven Speaks" booklets are now available in PDF format for free download and printing from our website www.directionforourtimes.org. We encourage everyone to print and distribute these booklets.

Other books by Anne, a lay apostle

Climbing the Mountain
Discovering your path to holiness
Anne's experiences of Heaven

The Mist of Mercy
Spiritual Warfare
Anne's experiences of Purgatory

Serving In Clarity
A Guide for Lay Apostles
of Jesus Christ the Returning King

In Defense of Obedience
and
Reflections on the Priesthood
Two Essays on topics close to the Heart of Jesus

Lessons in Love
Moving Toward Divine Intimacy

Interviews with Anne, a lay apostle

VHS tapes and DVDs featuring Anne, a lay apostle have been produced by Focus Worldwide Network and can be purchased by visiting our website at **www.directionforourtimes.org**